DISCUSSIONS:
A Guide To Navigating Healthcare Choices

Patsy Barnes

Gotham Books

30 N Gould St.
Ste. 20820, Sheridan, WY 82801
https://gothambooksinc.com/

Phone: 1 (307) 464-7800

© 2023 *Patsy Barnes*. All rights reserved.

No part of this book may be reproduced, stored in a retrieval system, or transmitted by any means without the written permission of the author.

Published by Gotham Books (July 28, 2023)

    ISBN: 979-8-88775-432-1 (P)
    ISBN: 979-8-88775-433-8 (E)

Because of the dynamic nature of the Internet, any web addresses or links contained in this book may have changed since publication and may no longer be valid.

The views expressed in this work are solely those of the author and do not necessarily reflect the views of the publisher, and the publisher hereby disclaims any responsibility for them.

TABLE OF CONTENTS

QUALITY OF LIFE ISSUES: 02
BENEFIT/BURDEN 06
TYPES OF CARE 09
PAIN MANAGEMENT 12
DEFINITIONS 15

    CPR- CARDIOPULMONARY RESUSCITATION 15
    VENTILATOR- MECHANICAL BREATHING 16
    FEEDING TUBES- ARTIFICIAL NUTRITION AND HYDRATION 17
    ANTIBIOTICS 18
    CHEMOTHERAPY 19
    DIALYSIS- KIDNEY MACHINE 20
    COMFORT CARE/ PALLIATIVE CARE 21

ADVANCED PLANNING 23

PREFACE

DISCUSSIONS: A GUIDE TO NAVIGATING HEALTHCARE CHOICES

This book was written after seeing many patients and families struggle with medical decisions. It is difficult to have conversations about potentially hard subjects, but the reason to have them when you are healthy and not under duress, is that, when the time comes, your family will not be stressed in deciding what treatments you do or do not want. The medical system has a language of its own and that does not make decisions easy. This book is a guide to those medical terms, as well as common treatments for chronic diseases, and the paperwork needed to make your wishes known.

The title of this booklet is "Discussions" because there is a real need to have some of these discussions when you are a complex or chronically ill patient. These need to take place between the patient and physician, the patient and family and the patient and caregivers. It is not enough to say that those close to you understand what you would want in certain situations.

It is amazing, although the subjects are difficult, that people handicap and burden others to make decisions about healthcare while never talking about these difficult topics. Some people feel that if they are discussed, then they will occur, much as people ignore talking about death, not wishing to "tempt it" into occurring.

Presented in this book are very difficult subjects, but very important subjects, that should be discussed more than once, and many should be ongoing discussions with caregivers and physicians. Many patients feel that if these discussions are so important, the doctor should bring them up and begin the talk. However, physicians are not trained to begin these discussions any more than patients are trained to do so and the lack of communication on so vital a subject as types of treatment choices, or feeding tubes can become critical decisions for others to make in chronically ill patients.

QUALITY OF LIFE ISSUES:

Quality of life issues revolve around the ability of the patient to maintain activities of daily living {ADL's}, meet the needs that they have for contributing to society and the benefit/burden ratio. Quality of life is based on the value system of the patient and what things matter to them in life, what makes life worth living. There are lots of considerations and factors involved including the energy level of the patient, ability to concentrate, ability to communicate, mobility to accomplish tasks, time conservation and energy conservation techniques available to patient, medications and side effects, ability to understand and process ideas and to make those thoughts known.

Quality of life changes, maybe drastically, in patients with chronic illness. Quality of life is purely subjective and based on the patient's values system. Some patients would say that they would never want to live in a wheelchair and then find themselves in exactly that position and their view of quality-of-life changes to adapt to their changing situation. Life satisfaction is very subjective and therefore, is very hard to measure. Without some guidance from the patient, medical caregivers interject their own quality of life ideas on patients and families. Often, families don't know what the patient would want for quality of life and are put into the position of making decisions without such knowledge. There is no "blood test" for quality of life, nor is it measurable or quantifiable. Consequently, without the patients input, it is hard to judge what treatment options should be considered. Chronically ill patients need to really examine their quality-of-life issues and how these change through the illness and with differing prognosis. These ideas need to be considered and then reevaluated often in chronically ill and complex patients. Quality of life issues are very personal and can make the difference between continuing certain treatments and reconsidering others. They are uniquely individual and based on the values system of the patient and family.

Balance is a key component in maintaining quality of life in patients with chronic diseases and each patient is charged with the task of finding that balance and what they can do to maintain their own unique balance in the daily living requirements of illness. It is a continuing cycle in that quality-of-life influences symptoms for better or worse and vice versa as symptoms influence the quality of life of complex patients. There is a bargaining part in quality of life for chronically ill patients. If the condition gets better and the quality of life gets better, then the patient will continue treatment at its current level. There is the burden/benefit discussion for quality of life. If the burden of treatment is less than the quality of life it affords then it might be worth the burden. If the quality of life isn't acceptable with the current treatment, than another may need to be considered, with less burden and more benefit. Each patient is responsible for making the decision of quality of life and what is acceptable and what is not and how treatment should proceed based on that knowledge.

Medications and medication regimes can have a big effect on quality of life. Taking 20 different pills several times daily with the resulting affects on bladder/bowel/stomach and level of consciousness make a case for being a knowledgeable and proactive patient. Is the pain medication causing too much nausea, or making the patient too tired and groggy to complete his ADL's? If one needs a "water pill" when do you take it? The timing, dosing and amount of medication can adversely affect a patients' quality of life. Palliative medicine, as referred to in another chapter, focuses care on using the least number of medications to control the symptoms of a patient. An amazing experiment for you, the proactive patient, would be to take your regular daily doses of medication in for the doctor to actually see the amount of energy it takes just to consume them, as well as distribute them during the day. One picture is worth a thousand words perhaps. Medications can also complicate one's quality of life by making the patient unable to focus their energy for tasks and decisions that need to be made. Again, there is a benefit/burden ratio to be considered. Are the medications giving enough benefit to the quality of a patients' life rather than creating more burden for those same activities? Each patient must make this decision and discuss it with the prescribing physician. Being a complex patient requires significant energy to complete simple tasks sometimes and for the complex patient, energy conservation is necessary.

There are a number of therapies which focus on assisting complex patients with simple daily tasks and energy conservation. The chronically ill lung patient can practice physical exercises to expand their chest muscles and aid in breathing. There are techniques for making dyspnea, or shortness of breath, bearable for the patients and their families. There are transfer techniques and physical exercises to strengthen ancillary muscles needed in walking and talking, as well as eating. Good sleep is also necessary in order to make good decisions and even though being a complex, chronically ill patient uses great energy and exhausts the patient, good sleep is a pattern and requires attention be paid to it for the good of the patient and family. It is difficult for those caring for patients to have their sleep patterns interrupted, as caregiving requires exceptional amounts of energy. Care, time, and attention should be paid to caregivers and their needs as part of the quality-of-life discussions of the patient.

BENEFIT/BURDEN

In all chronically ill patients, there is a benefit/burden ratio that begins at time of diagnosis and continues through all phases of treatment, whether acute or palliative care model. The ratio is based on the benefit the patient, family and caregivers will receive from the particular treatment versus the burden placed on the patient as well as family and caregivers. It is important to realize that the patient is not the only part of the equation of benefit/burden. Often the medical system per se focuses on the patient, but certainly those around the patient, whether caregivers or family, which may be one in the same, must be taken into consideration.

Early in the diagnosis of a chronic disease, the benefit side usually outweighs the burden. Treatments in acute care medicine often alleviate the troubling symptoms and the exacerbation of the illness is eased. As stated in an earlier part of this booklet, chronic illness' are marked by times of feeling good and then times of exacerbations of the disease. Increased shortness of breath in the chronic lung patient is an example. These exacerbations usually end with the patient being admitted to the acute care hospital for symptom management. Early in diagnosis, these "bad" times may be few and far between. However, as chronic disease progresses, the benefit/burden ratio changes and needs to be addressed as part of the treatment goals.

Only the patient and those involved with the patient can decide when the exacerbations are becoming more burden than benefit. This decision is based on the patients' value system.

Benefit/burden applies to both the patient and significant others involved with the patient. In acute care medicine, the benefit/burden ratio takes a secondary place in the treatment process, as the goal is curative. Sometimes, as in the case of chemotherapy, there is a burden up front, but the benefit stands to outweigh the temporary burden. However, in the chronically ill patient the treatment plan needs to include the benefit/burden ratio as a primary part of the treatment plan and needs to be addressed on an ongoing basis. This process is very difficult for those physicians trained in only acute care medicine. To address the ongoing burden to the patient and family in relationship to the benefit is often hidden or completely ignored in the medical model. There is an accompanying feeling of failure on the part of the physician, which is uncomfortable at best and miserable at most, so that the medical system chooses to ignore this benefit/burden ratio completely. Chronically ill/complex patients cannot afford to ignore this ratio and those physicians that regularly treat chronically ill/complex patients recognize this importance. Once the discussion is begun, to revisit it is easier and patients will be aware of the shifting of the benefit/burden choices that are available to them. Included in this conversation should be the quality-of-life issues addressed earlier in this pamphlet.

As the benefit/burden ratio changes, treatment choices should also be addressed and realistic goals for treatment included. What treatment a patient chooses may change over time, with exacerbations of the disease and with the shifting of the benefits and burdens of each treatment choice. Physicians rarely understand the amount of energy it takes to be chronically ill and the amount of physical as well as psychological energy needed to recover back to a level of quality of life that is still acceptable to a patient. Over time, and with each exacerbation of the disease, the patient loses a bit in the recovery. They never quite gets back up to the previous acceptable quality of life. Contrary to the acute care model of medicine whose patients return to a previously acceptable quality of life, or even better quality, the chronically ill patient doesn't have this same advantage. Patients in the acute tract of medicine usually experience a life altering event, are treated in the acute care model, and go back to a level of function very close to their baseline. That is not true of the chronically ill/complex patient, whose recovery may be more energy and emotionally taxing; this on a body system that is already being tried on a daily basis. Living with a chronic illness is not for sissies.

TYPES OF CARE

Acute care is directed toward aggressive treatment leading to a cure of disease. It involves technology and medications, as well as diagnostic tests and perhaps surgery or other procedures focusing on the cure of disease. Acute care focuses on the patient and does not always lend itself to the care of those associated with the patient, i.e., family, caregivers, significant others. Acute care decisions may include members of the healthcare team and patient and families, but ultimately the decision rests with the patient in the acute care setting. Acute care medicine is wonderful for those diseases and injuries that can be cured. Heart attacks, strokes, pneumonia, and trauma injuries are among the disease processes that are well managed in the acute care medical system. However, as society ages, there becomes a large number of people diagnosed with chronic disease processes, which have periods of effective management and periods of difficulty. These times when the disease gets worse are called exacerbations of disease. The patient does well for a long period of time and then experiences a period of difficulty, brought on by certain "triggers" of sorts and usually the patient finds their way to the acute care hospital. Acute care medicine can alleviate or at least moderate the symptoms of chronic disease but cannot cure the disease itself. Diagnosis of congestive heart failure, chronic obstructive pulmonary disease, diabetes, and arthritis are examples of chronic illness that have periods of exacerbations. For these types of disease, palliative care medicine has become the gold standard in medicine.

Palliative care is the aggressive treatment of symptoms of chronic disease processes with the emphasis not on cure, but on patient comfort and quality of life. Palliative care may include some diagnostic tests, but the focus is not on cure, but rather better control of symptoms that lead to multiple and long hospitalizations. Palliative care focuses on the patient, family and caregivers as a unit to be cared for, not just the patient alone. Shared decision making is the hallmark of palliative care, where the patient, family and caregivers are all included in the treatment planning and realistic goal setting. Palliative care is making great strides in the area of pain management, which is an area that causes great difficulty and miscommunication in patients who are complex or have rare disease processes. The World Health Organization defines palliative care as "the active, total care of patients whose disease is not responsive to curative treatment. Control of pain, of other symptoms, and of psychological, social, and spiritual problems is paramount. The goal of palliative care is the achievement of the best possible quality of life for patients and their families." Goals of palliative care include realistic goals for patients, families and caregivers, discussion of values and the patients' narrative, acceptable and unacceptable quality of life, advanced planning, benefit/burden ratio and shared decision making. Palliative care is actually "old" medicine, before the time of technology and life extension in chronically ill patients, before the need for discussion of "how much" is "too much."

Hospice care is defined by the Medicare benefit that financially pays for end-of-life care with the requirement that the patient be within 6 months of death. However, as long as the patients' condition is deteriorating, hospice care can continue past the 6-month time frame. Hospice care focuses on the comfort of the dying patient, care for the family and caregivers and emotional and spiritual care after the death of the patient. Hospice caregivers have their emphasis on patient comfort at end of life specifically and the symptoms that cause problems for dying patients and their families. Sleep deprivation, artificial feeding, and advance planning for end of life are paramount in the hospice model. Prior to this time in medicine, patients went from the acute care model right to the hospice model, but with the palliative care model gaining credibility in the medical system, there may be large numbers of patients who will be better served with palliative care for years before entering into the hospice example at end of life. Both palliative and hospice care models have quality of life as the foremost benefit to patients and families. Acute care medicine does not always address that particular discussion because acute care medicine might actually make a patient's quality of life worse in order to make it better with time and treatment.

PAIN MANAGEMENT

Ever since the SUPPORT study, a 10-year study of people at the end of life in America was published, the idea of better pain management has become central in medicine. JCAHO, the joint commission on accreditation of hospital organization made pain management one of its focus issues in the past 6-8 years. All medical facilities had increased education for medical staff and ancillary personnel. The object was to better manage patients' pain while ill or hospitalized. New technologies such as patient administered IV pain medications and epidural pain medication delivery moved toward patient comfort, but the problem of abuse of narcotic pain medication continues to plague healthcare professionals. There is no blood test for pain levels and the old standby of a pain shot every 4 hours in the thigh or buttocks isn't the standard anymore. Sadly, all of the focus has not made pain management any better for patients, especially those with chronic and ongoing pain. There are pain management specialty physicians, but few of them and even fewer in the rural areas. Listed as one of the rights of patients, good pain management is often neglected and ruled still by misconceptions on the part of care givers and patients alike.

Medicine changes very slowly. In order to better manage pain, the patient must be clear about the rights and responsibilities of being a patient. With chronic pain, a request for a pain specialist can certainly be accommodated and the patient must then be very clear about the pain they are having. Pain management specialists have certainly helped in this area, but the medications lend themselves to such abuse by some patients, that the healthcare provider often feels that they are supplying addicts rather than treating the patients pain appropriately. Sadly, the patients with pain run head long into a system that sees the need for pain medication abused and that physicians have been prosecuted for, in fact, prescribing the appropriate medications and dosages. Palliative care and hospice care have been the longstanding torchbearers for good pain control and management.

There are a few points about pain management that should be discussed with family and friends, especially for chronically ill/complex patients. The amount of pain medication, usually a narcotic, will make patients very sleepy and sometimes even somnolent or comatose. How important it is to a patient to have their pain managed and what level of pain they are willing to endure to be awake and alert is a big question. It is the old benefit/burden ratio. Some patients will want their pain treated to the utmost and are willing to be sleepy during the daytime and miss out on any visits or activities that may come about. Other patients may be willing to endure a bit more pain in the waking hours so as to accomplish some goal or remain alert to their living situation. Again, this is a patient choice, but must be discussed and made clear with those persons who will have to make decisions if the patient is too sleepy or not alert enough to make decisions.

Another very important point of discussion is something called "terminal sedation" for lack of a better term. This is usually accomplished by a hospice trained or palliative care trained clinician and means that the patient will be kept unconscious to alleviate suffering, such as pain that cannot be controlled, or constant seizures that do not respond to medication. This drastic step of "terminal sedation" is usually reserved for those close to end of life and who have chosen this option as opposed to being awake and suffering severe pain or other symptoms.

DEFINITIONS

We, in the medical profession, use terms that we throw around as though everyone knows and understands their full implications. The sad truth is that most people have some knowledge of these terms, but don't fully understand the full extent of each treatment and its meaning about the health or illness of the individual. Here are seven common medical treatments and what they are like.

CPR- CARDIOPULMONARY RESUSCITATION

DEFINITION: An emergency procedure that attempts to restore and maintain breathing and circulation in a person whose heart or breathing has stopped.

DESCRIPTION: CPR includes the following methods: forceful compressions of the chest over the heart: assisted breathing through a tube in the windpipe attached to a ventilator, or a handheld breathing bag connected to a mask that is placed over the mouth and nose: intravenous medications: electric shock once or repeatedly.

BENEFITS: Survival rate and return to previous condition can be high in a previously healthy person if CPR is begun immediately.

BURDEN: Less successful with older adults and people with chronic conditions or if CPR is delayed. When breathing stops, oxygen doesn't reach a person's brain which may cause brain damage and lead to a range of disabilities. Brain damage can occur within a few minutes. Forceful pumping on the chest can cause later pain, broken ribs or breastbone, cuts or bruises of the spleen or liver, or rupture of a lung.

VENTILATOR- MECHANICAL BREATHING

DEFINITION: Breathing with the help of a machine. A ventilator is also called a "respirator."

DESCRIPTION: A machine that helps a person breathe when he or she is unable to do so on his own. For short term conditions [after an accident or surgery] a tube is placed either in the mouth or nose and into the patient's windpipe. Medication is often used to ease the discomfort during this procedure. For a long-term condition [more than one month] a tube may be placed directly into a hole that has been surgically created in the patient's windpipe. This procedure is called a "tracheostomy." In a hospital, ventilators are powered by generators so that they continue to function even if there is a loss of the central power supply.

BENEFITS: May only be needed on a short-term basis, following surgery or until the patient can breathe on his own. There are people with disabilities who live with ongoing ventilator support.

BURDEN: A nose or mouth tube is uncomfortable and makes it impossible to speak or eat. Pneumonia and other infections are possible, as are sinus infections, mouth wounds and dry mouth. With a tracheostomy, speaking may be limited to very short periods of time. The long-term burden is the inability to be "weaned off" the ventilator, or breath on the patients own which will then require someone to make the decision to "pull the plug" on the ventilator.

FEEDING TUBES- ARTIFICIAL NUTRITION AND HYDRATION

DEFINITION: A method of providing nutrition and fluids through a tube, for a patient who cannot eat or drink normally. Also called "tube feeding".

DESCRIPTION: There are two methods of tube feeding. Nutrition in liquid form can be given through a small flexible tube passed through the nose to the stomach, or the liquid can be delivered directly to the stomach through a tube that has been surgically inserted by way of the abdomen commonly called a " G tube or J tube." The surgical route is usually used when the feeding will be long term, or when there is a trauma to the mouth, throat, or face that makes a nose tube difficult. It may be needed on a temporary or permanent basis. There is another way of feeding patients which is IV or through tubes into the central circulatory system. Called "TPN", it is usually a short-term treatment for patients whose GI, or stomach system, cannot utilize the liquid food used in the "feeding tubes".

BENEFITS: The ability to prolong life by providing liquids, calories, and minerals needed to maintain internal bodily functions. Artificial nutrition can help a person through a period of recovery, sustaining life and helping healing. A stomach tube reduces the risk of the patient accidentally getting nutritional fluids into the lungs. The standard living will form has a place to indicate whether the patient would want a feeding tube placed and under what conditions they would not want artificial nutrition and hydration. There are several religious beliefs that have very important stands on the issue of artificial nutrition and hydration.

BURDENS: The nose tube can make talking and swallowing uncomfortable; it can also cause sores and irritation in the nose. It is possible that an infection can develop at the site of the stomach tube put in from the abdomen. For patients with a terminal condition, the tube feeding may cause abdominal distension and discomfort as the patients body cannot utilize the food or fluids in its terminal state.

ANTIBIOTICS

Once viewed as the savior of modern medicine, antibiotics have proven to be controversial.

Definition: Medications to combat serious infections anywhere in the body. Pneumonia and urinary tract infections are examples.

DESCRIPTION: Antibiotics are usually administered in pill or liquid form or through IV forms. Many more bacteria are becoming resistant to the usual antibiotic regime and for chronically ill patients; these antibiotics may be very powerful.

BENEFITS: Antibiotics can cure a serious infection easing discomfort from fever or pain.

BURDENS: Antibiotics treat infection but do not correct the underlying health problems and may in fact, prolong the patients dying process. Infection may be the cause of death in terminal or debilitated patients.

CHEMOTHERAPY

DEFINITION: Administration of drugs to fight cancer. The goal is to destroy malignant [cancerous or harmful] tumor cells without causing excessive or irreversible damage to the patient's normal cells.

DESCRIPTION: Drugs are administered either in pill form or through an injection or through an IV [intravenous] tube. Chemotherapy can be done in a doctor's office, hospital, outpatient setting or in the patients' home.

BENEFITS: It is possible that the cancer cells will be destroyed. Chronic diseases can go into remission or even be cured. Chemotherapy has become a standard in the acute care medical system.

BURDENS: The side effects may include hair loss, nausea, vomiting, sores in the mouth, throat and intestines, loss of appetite, fatigue, anemia, bleeding, and higher susceptibility to infections. There are drugs that may minimize or prevent some of these risks.

The burdens of chemotherapy may be great and should be measured along with the benefits of the course of chemotherapy. If a few months of burden can manage several years of benefit, then the treatment may be worth the effort. If, however, the burden of the chemotherapy will only add to the suffering and not to the mortality of the patient, then discussion should take place about the patients' wishes at end of life.

DIALYSIS- KIDNEY MACHINE

DESCRIPTION: The cleaning of the blood by a machine for patients whose kidneys have failed. Dialysis offers an artificial mechanism for performing some kidney functions.

DEFINITION: Inserting large tubes through the arm or groin and into large blood vessels and attaching them to a portable machine that cleans the blood of excess chemicals, minerals, and impurities and removes excess fluid. Dialysis treatments usually take 2-4 hours: may be needed as often as daily and can be done in a hospital or outpatient setting. Dialysis may be needed for a temporary period, or it may be needed permanently.

BENEFITS: It can assume kidney function for the body while the kidneys have time to recover or while waiting for a kidney transplant.

BURDENS: Dialysis does not cure the underlying kidney condition. If the kidneys don't recover, the patient may need to rely on dialysis forever. Complications of long-term dialysis include anemia that may require blood transfusions, moderate skin itching and fatigue. Repeated surgery to insert new tubes into the arm or groin is often necessary. Diet must be strictly regulated, and people must remain near dialysis facilities at all times.

COMFORT CARE/ PALLIATIVE CARE

DEFINITION: A range of treatments intended to relieve pain and suffering, control adverse symptoms, reduce anxiety and provide comprehensive support for the patient, family, and caregivers.

DESCRIPTION: Palliative care includes the following: administering pain medicine, hygiene [mouth care and bathing the patient], temperature control, massage, bringing drinks, changing bed linens, turning the patient, hand holding, stroking, and emotional support for the family, friends and other medical staff, and spiritual support from hospital chaplains and personal religious advisors. It can also include providing soothing diversions such as music and aroma.

BENEFITS: Comfort care reduces pain and discomfort. It provides emotional support for both patient and family and helps create a peaceful and nurturant environment for all concerned.

BURDENS: Comfort care does not correct the underlying physical disease process and does not address curative treatments or the acute care model.

ADVANCED PLANNING

Perhaps there is no more important part in the process of disease, whether chronic illness or sudden onset acute illness, that assists both the patient and medical system like advanced planning. This allows the patient to state his values and desires for treatment and refusal of treatment according to that values system. It gives direction to the medical team, as well as direction to those people close to the patient and those who might have to speak for the patient in the event the patient cannot speak for themself. This eases the burden placed on the family or friends of the patient. This single act of advanced planning can make difficult decisions easier for those making them for an unconscious patient as well as allow the medical team to honor those same wishes.

There are multiple different forms needed for advanced planning.
- MDPOA – medical durable power of attorney
- Living will
- State Do Not Resuscitate form or DNR order

However, the most important thing is to talk to family and friends and healthcare providers about realistic treatment goals and goals of end-of-life care when patient may not be able to speak for himself/herself. The patient should discuss what things make life good and worth living and what things or conditions are not to be tolerated. There are multiple gray areas in advanced planning, so the need for communication as the disease process changes is very important and as goals for treatment change. The patient must communicate his values to those who will be charged with making decisions when the patient is unable to do so.

A medical durable power of attorney [MDPOA] authorizes a named person to make medical decisions for the patient when the patient is unable to do so. It carries no financial implications, but rather specifies what decisions the person can make on behalf of the patient. It becomes binding only when the patient cannot speak for themself and ends when the patient can again speak for themselves and make their own decisions. These decisions are medical in nature only and the power of attorney only lasts as long as the patient is unable to speak for themselves. The MDPOA cannot go against any stated wishes that the patient left before becoming unable to speak for themselves. The following scenario is all too well known to caregivers in the acute care system. The patient has left specific directions about end-of-life care and when the patient becomes unable to speak for himself, the medical durable power of attorney begins to make demands that go against the expressed written directions of the patient. The physician is caught between honoring the patients expressed wishes and the lawsuit threatened by the person speaking for the patient. That is why it is so important to discuss wishes for treatment and refusal of treatment with the person you designate as your MDPOA. Properly written advanced directives made by the patient should be honored at all times as being the voice of the patient directly and the MDPOA is expected to abide by those wishes. However, at times of crisis, there are feelings of guilt and desires on the part of the MDPOA that are not what the patient designated as his/her wishes. When naming the person to speak for you, consider the difficulty of the decisions that will need to be made and select someone who has the courage to stand up and advocate for you and also, consider someone who will be already in an emotionally upset state and adding to that burden, the burden of making important medical decisions and treatment choices. One's MDPOA must be someone who knows the importance of the patient's values and can also state those to the medical system. The standard MDPOA forms can be downloaded on the internet and do not require a physician's signature or a lawyer to execute the document. They do usually require a witness to the patients' signature and should not be anyone that could benefit from the patient's poor outcome.

A living will states under what conditions life saving equipment and technology may be removed from a patient who cannot speak for themselves. The document does not state for technology or life sustaining machinery not to be instituted, but merely under what circumstances it should be removed. Many patients think that because they have a living will, that CPR will not be instituted, and they are quite wrong. There are several problems with the standard living will. It usually states that two physicians must agree that the patient has a terminal illness. The problem is that a stroke, or an accident resulting in brain damage is not considered a terminal illness. In fact, there are very few terminal illness's that were prevalent during the 1970's when living wills became prominent. Pneumonia, which is the cause of death for many debilitated patients is not considered a terminal illness and the patient may be treated for sepsis, which is a systemic infection multiple time. There is usually a time limit on the removal of life sustaining machinery, but the number of days may not reflect the patient's true status.

There is also a place on the living will to state the wishes for artificial nutrition/hydration to be considered or not, according to the patients values and desires. It does not take into consideration the temporary need for a feeding tube for best recovery and is therefore, a problem area also Sometimes patients are unable to swallow temporarily or require a feeding tube to allow enough calories for optimal healing and the living will does not distinguish between these conditions. Therefore, it is essential that the MDPOA knows the patients desires for artificial nutrition and hydration. The living will doesn't require a physician's signature, but usually requires a witness to the patient's signature and does not require a lawyer to execute. Standard Living will forms can be downloaded from the internet.

Most states have a standard physicians order for Do Not Resuscitate or Do Not Attempt Resuscitation. This means that, in the event of a heart or lung malfunction or stoppage, that CPR will not be started, or life saving/sustaining technology will not be instituted Some patients who have living wills think that they have this kind of document and are sadly mistaken.   CPR directives or DNR orders must be signed by the physician and patient with the understanding that death may ensue if the paper is followed.   This type of advanced directive must usually be obtained from a physician's office and is a legal document. It requires the signature of both physician and patient and should take place only after a discussion on the ramifications of executing such a document. It is very important that, if you have a DNR order or state CPR Directive that you make the EMS personnel aware of it and that it be posted in an obvious place in the bedroom and also on the refrigerator door. Most EMS personnel will look at those two places when it is known that a patient has such a paper.   You, as a proactive patient, should notify the closest EMS providers who would most likely respond to a 911 call from your house.

Obviously, making advanced plans is an important part of your treatment and care as a complex, chronically ill patient. There are several ways to make these wishes known and one of those is the 5 Wishes Booklet.   It contains several papers, including the MDPOA form and living will form.   It does not contain a CPR directive or DNR form, as those require a physician's signature. However, the 5 Wishes Booklet makes advance planning easier and gives several scenarios that might make decisions more clear.   Advanced planning also makes the burden on those left to make difficult decisions lighter.

Technology and advanced medical practices have made these decisions very difficult and emotionally trying for those left to make them when the patient cannot. To insure that your wishes are abided by a proactive patient should have the appropriate papers and discussions with their family and friends. This is one way of assuring you, as a patient with a debilitating illness, that you will be heard when times are difficult and there are choices to be made about treatment or refusal of treatment.

There is a relatively new form in many states that allows yet more discussions and healthcare choices. It comes with different names in different states, but the choices and information is the same. It can be called the MOST< MOLST< POST or POLST form depending on your particular state. The acronym stands for "physician's order/medical order for life-sustaining treatment, this form is intended to be used by the chronically or seriously ill person in frequent contact with healthcare providers or already residing in a nursing facility. This form has become a required form for most long term care facilities. It is a legal document and requires a signature from a medical provider, either a doctor, physician's assistant, or nurse practitioner.

The form addresses, in one document, the CPR directive, choices about acute care, comfort care and hospice case, as well as choices about antibiotics, artificial nutrition and hydration and hospitalization. The great advantage of this form is that if follows the patient through the entire healthcare system, from home, to hospital, to rehab facility and to long term care. The form can be and should be amended as the disease progresses. The form DOES NOT ADDRESS THE MDPOA. That form needs to be separate although the named MDPOA could be and should be part of the decisions made on the form.

The most important advance directive a patient can have is the MDPOA paper that names someone to speak for you when you are unable to do so.

30

www.ingramcontent.com/pod-product-compliance
Lightning Source LLC
LaVergne TN
LVHW051923060526
838201LV00060B/4151